Craft It Up
Around the World

Craft It Up
Around the World

35 FUN CRAFT PROJECTS
INSPIRED BY TRAVELING ADVENTURES

LIBBY ABADEE
AND CATH ARMSTRONG

CICO kidz

From Libby:
*For Phil and our beautiful children,
Angus, India, Jack, Gracie, and Emily.*

From Cath:
*For Ray and my children, Caitlin, Nicholas,
and Marcus, who inspire me daily.*

Published in 2013 by CICO Kidz
An imprint of Ryland Peters & Small
519 Broadway, 5th Floor, New York NY 10012
20–21 Jockey's Fields, London WC1R 4BW
www.rylandpeters.com

10 9 8 7 6 5 4 3 2 1

Text copyright © Libby Abadee and Cath Armstrong 2013
Design, step photography, and project photography
copyright © CICO Books 2013
For picture credits for additional photography and
illustration, see page 128.

A CIP catalog record for this book is available from the
Library of Congress and the British Library.

ISBN: 978-1-78249-038-8

Printed in China

Editor: Lindsay Kaubi
Designer: Mark Latter
Photographer: Cath Armstrong
Templates: Simon Roulstone

Contents

Introduction

The whole world is on our doorstep. You can step onto a plane and fly far away from home; you can pick up a beautiful book of photographs, watch an amazing documentary, or surf the world on the Internet.

We are both passionate world travelers. Between us we have lived in places far and wide, from the crumbling Victorian streets of England to the vibrant and wonderful city of Sydney, Australia, via the hot, sandy deserts of Saudi Arabia and the flat plains of Kansas, USA.

This book combines our love of the cities we have lived in, visited, or just dreamed about and the crafts that are inspired by the world beyond our front door.

We want you to be inspired by your own journeys, either real or imagined, and create beautiful crafts to capture your adventures.

Go to the library and get out a book with big, glossy photos; plan a trip; search through travel blogs on the Internet; have big dreams and even bigger plans. And when you return from your trip or your reading, why don't you make some salt dough coins to evoke the magic of the Trevi Fountain? Or make a Times Square pencil tin to store your holiday magnets in? Give the whirling dervish doll a spin, or banish worries with our "No Worries" worry dolls inspired by Peru? There is magic in remembering adventures of a lifetime, and we hope that these projects will keep the magic alive or inspire you to dream and travel.

Enjoy!

Cath & Libby

NORTH
AMERICA

SOUTH
AMERICA

ANTARCTICA

EUROPE

ASIA

AFRICA

OCEANIA

Map of the World

1 ANTARCTICA

THE AMERICAS
2 *Argentina*
3 *Brazil*
4 *Canada*
5 *Colombia*
6 *Cuba*
7 *Jamaica*
8 *Mexico*
9 *Peru*
10 *United States of America*

EUROPE
11 *Austria*
12 *Finland*
13 *France*
14 *Greece*
15 *Hungary*
16 *Italy*
17 *Netherlands*
18 *Russia*
19 *Spain*
20 *Sweden*
21 *Turkey*
22 *United Kingdom*

ASIA AND OCEANIA
23 *Australia*
24 *China*
25 *India*
26 *Indonesia*
27 *Japan*
28 *New Zealand*
29 *Saudi Arabia*
30 *United Arab Emirates*
31 *Vietnam*

AFRICA
32 *Egypt*
33 *Ghana*

"I'd Like to Teach the World to String" Map Bunting

There are a million beautiful things you can do with a map. In this project you could identify places you've visited and cut them out to make them a part of your bunting — or even use places you've only read about or would like to visit.

YOU WILL NEED

Circle punch or a pencil, scissors, and a glass

Map

Sewing machine

Thread

1. A circle punch, available from craft stores, was used to cut out these circles from a map; however, if you don't have one, you could just use a glass as a template, draw around it, and cut out the circles with scissors.

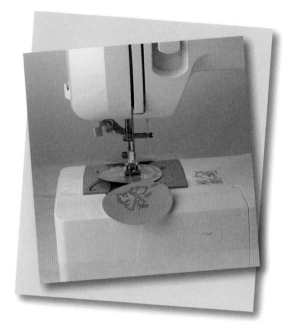

2. You need a sewing machine for the next step. Gently pull about 10in (25cm) of thread from the sewing machine before you start. You can make this into a loop to hang your bunting when you have finished. Gently start feeding your circles into the sewing machine so that you sew through the center of each circle, joining it to the previous one—as soon as you have sewn across one circle, start to feed the next in so that they just touch. White thread was used here, but any color would do.

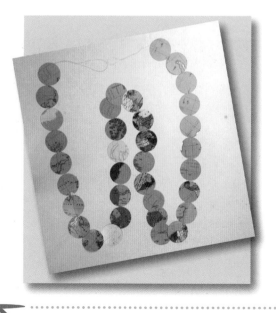

3. When you have sewn all of your circles, gently pull out another 10in (25cm) of thread. Make the two ends of thread into loops by tying them in a knot.

Chapter 1
The Americas
and Antarctica

It's no coincidence that America is known as a "melting pot." The Americas are rich with diversity, from colorful Mexican sombreros to the bright lights of Times Square in New York City. Come and fly with our beautiful Brazilian butterflies (see page 18), or march off with a Canadian Mountie gingerbread man (see page 22).

Bag Yourself a Potato Print Tote

ARGENTINA

Using potatoes to print on fabric gives a lovely, slightly mottled effect — similar to colorful ikat fabric, which is popular in South America (see Fun Fact, page 15). To get really crisp-edged designs you can cut your potatoes with a sharp cookie cutter. For this project, we used a sharp knife and a template, so you need to be careful while you are cutting or ask an adult to help with this step. No measuring is necessary for this design. If you start in the center and work outward, then the pattern will be centered. Overlapping only adds to the overall effect!

YOU WILL NEED

Muslin bag (ironed, if necessary)

Paper, pen and scissors to make the templates

1 large potato

Sharp knife

Tea towel

3 different colors of fabric paint

Large ceramic or glass plate

Parchment or baking paper cut to the size of your bag

Iron for setting the paint

ARGENTINIAN FLAG

1. Draw a template for your large diamond and one for your small diamond on the paper and cut them out. The large diamonds measure 1¾in (4.5cm) across and 2⅜in (6cm) down. The small ones are 1in (2.5cm) across and 1⅛in (3cm) down. You may want to make them smaller or larger depending on the size of your bag.

2. Slip your parchment paper inside the bag. This will stop the fabric paint from going through to the other side of the bag. Lightly fold the bag so that you can see where the middle is. This is where your design will start.

3. Cut your potato in half and place your large template on one half. Using a sharp knife cut the potato into the diamond shape. Repeat this step with the smaller template. Blot your potatoes on a tea towel to dry them out.

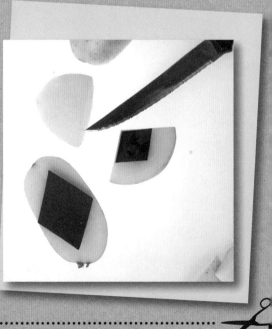

4. Dip your potatoes in fabric paint and print rows of large diamonds first, tessellating each row as you go. We used a repeating pattern but you could create a random pattern or use more colors. When you want to change color, rinse your potato under a tap and then blot it dry before using it again. Allow the fabric paint to dry.

5. Once the first layer of diamonds is dry, stamp your smaller diamonds over the top. Allow all of the fabric paint to dry completely, and then iron according to manufacturer's instructions to set the paint.

fun fact

Ikat fabric has been popular in South America for centuries. It is made by a process similar to tie-dyeing. However, ikat textiles are made by dyeing the threads before they are woven, rather than by tie-dyeing the fabric.

REPUBLICA ARGENTINA

1 PESO

"In Awe of Aurora" Print

Here we have recreated the magic of the Southern Lights with a simple print. By changing the colors and the template you could make an outback sunrise scene or a sunset over the horizon.

1. Trace the templates on page 121 onto paper, draw around them on cardboard, and then cut them out. Use a ruler to mark out a border on your card stock—make sure that it is not bigger than your sheet of diffusing paper. Position your cardboard templates on the card stock and trace around them. Cut out your drawing to create your silhouette.

fun fact

The Aurora Australis, or Southern Lights, is a spectacular light show in the sky, which is created by nature. Energetic particles enter the atmosphere from above, creating a luminous, multicolored glow in the sky.

2. Using the water-based markers, draw wavy lines over your diffusing paper. It works best if you draw lots of them close together.

ANTARCTICA

Antarctica is not actually part of the Americas and is its own continent, although it is geographically closer to South America than anywhere else. It is the world's southernmost continent, containing the South Pole and surrounded by the Southern Ocean. It is nearly twice the size of Australia!

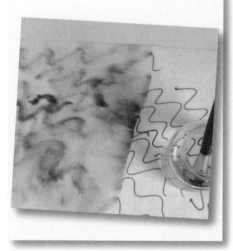

3. Paint water over the diffusing paper you have decorated with lines and allow the color to spread and dry.

4. Attach the diffusing paper to the back of your card stock with tape and place the finished piece on your wall or window.

A Flutter of Color

BRAZIL

Coffee filter papers are not just for making coffee! They are fabulous for craft activities and we have put them to great use in making these colored magnets, which you can use to stick things to the refrigerator.

ABOVE
Iguazu Falls, which lie between Brazil, Argentina, and Paraguay.

YOU WILL NEED

Florists' wire
2 wooden dolly clothespins
Glue
Acrylic paints of your color choice
Paintbrush
Black permanent marker
Coffee filter papers (large and small)
Paper towel
Food coloring
Magnet

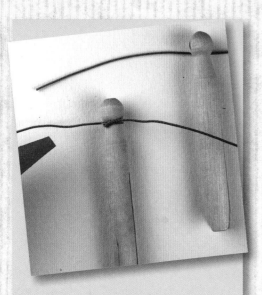

1. Cut a length of florists' wire in half and wrap it once around the neck of a dolly clothespin. Twist it, and secure it with a small dab of glue to the back of the clothespin.

2. Paint your clothespins. Be sure to paint in between the clothespin legs because the bottom part will remain visible. Allow the paint to dry and then, using a permanent black pen, mark in facial details such as eyes and mouth.

3. Use an extra dolly clothespin to curl the florists' wire you have attached to the first two clothespins to make butterfly antenna shapes.

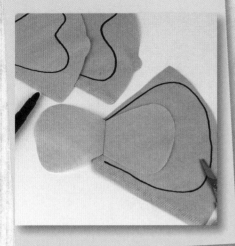

4. Take two coffee filters and on one draw a large wing and on the other draw a smaller wing of the same design. Cut them out leaving the bottom join of the coffee filter paper intact.

BRAZILIAN FLAG

5. Put your filter papers on the paper towel and place drops of food coloring onto the opened papers. Keep the design symmetrical by doing the same to both sides. Repeat the process for your smaller butterfly wings.

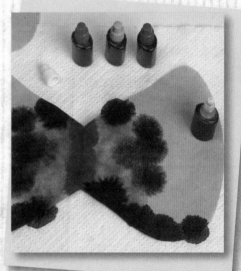

6. When the colored papers are dry, place the wings together and push them up between the clothespin legs. Glue a magnet on the back of the clothespin.

fun fact

The area of Iguaza Falls—where the countries of Argentina, Paraguay, and Brazil meet—is one of the best places in the world to see butterflies.

"The Mounties Always Get Their (Gingerbread) Man"

CANADA

Making gingerbread is one of our all-time favorite activities. From the mixing bowl and the sweet smell filling the house to the decorating and eating, each step is wonderful. In many countries gingerbread is traditional at Christmas but we think it should be made all year round! Let your imagination run wild with your shapes and icing designs. Visit a specialty store or craft store for unusual icing colors, or try and mix the supermarket ones into surprising shades.

RIGHT
Niagara Falls lies between the Canadian and the US border.

YOU WILL NEED

FOR THE DOUGH
(which makes roughly
12–15 gingerbread men):

2 cups (10oz/300g) flour

½ tsp baking soda

1 tbsp ground ginger

1 cup (12oz/350g) brown
sugar

1 egg

⅝ cup (5½oz/150g) softened
butter

Parchment paper

Rolling pin

Gingerbread man cookie cutter

Baking sheet

Cooling rack

Spatula

1 cup (4½oz/125g)
pure confectioner's sugar

3 cereal-size bowls

Black, red, and yellow food dye

½ cup (8fl oz/240ml) of water

3 teaspoons

Blunt butter knife

Toothpick

1. Preheat the oven to 325°F (170°C/Gas 3). Mix your dry ingredients together, and then add the egg and butter and mix until dough is formed. This step is much quicker if you can use an electric mixer with a dough hook. Roll out your dough between two sheets of parchment paper until the dough is roughly ⅜in (7mm) thick.

2. Line the baking sheet with parchment paper. Remove the top sheet of paper from your rolled out dough. Use your cutter to cut out your gingerbread men, and then transfer them to your baking sheet. Bake the gingerbread men for seven to 10 minutes or until they are golden. Transfer them to the cooling rack with spatula and allow to cool.

fun fact

Women only became regular members of the Royal Canadian Mounted Police in 1974.

CANADIAN FLAG

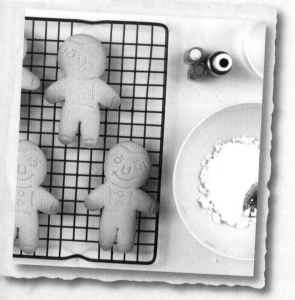

3. Divide 1 cup (4½oz/125g) of confectioner's sugar between three bowls. Add 10 drops of your red food coloring into one bowl, five drops of yellow into the next, and three drops of black into the last one. Gently add water to each bowl, stirring each with a teaspoon until the icing is stiff but spreadable.

4. Using the blunt butter knife spread some red icing onto the bodies of the gingerbread men. Then add the black boots with the black icing and the yellow cap with the yellow icing. Use a toothpick to draw the eyes, mouth, and belt, wiping it clean between colors. Make more icing as needed. Allow to set.

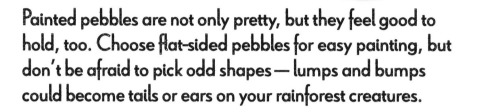

Rainforest
Painted Pebbles

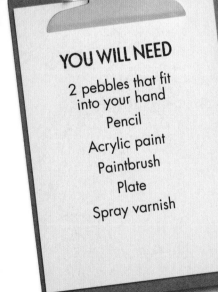

COLOMBIA

Painted pebbles are not only pretty, but they feel good to hold, too. Choose flat-sided pebbles for easy painting, but don't be afraid to pick odd shapes — lumps and bumps could become tails or ears on your rainforest creatures.

1. Choose your pebbles and clean them prior to painting. Our pebbles were about 2⅜in (6cm) across. Look through books or photographs on the Internet to find inspiration for rainforest wildlife. The frog and the toucan are two vibrant examples. Use a pencil to sketch your animal onto your pebble.

YOU WILL NEED

2 pebbles that fit into your hand
Pencil
Acrylic paint
Paintbrush
Plate
Spray varnish

fun fact

The Amazon rainforest spans nine countries of South America: Brazil, Peru, Colombia, Venezuela, Ecuador, Bolivia, Guyana, Suriname, and French Guiana. Brazil is home to the largest part of the Amazon rainforest, while about 10 percent of the rainforest is in Colombia.

2. Choose a background color that makes your animal stand out. Bright colors work really well. Paint the underside of your pebble with your background color. You may need to do more than one coat to get the depth of color you want. Place on a plate and allow the paint to dry.

COLOMBIAN FLAG

3. Flip over your pebble and start painting on top of your pencil sketch. Make sure the background color joins up with the underside of the pebble. Allow the paint to dry and spray the pebble with varnish, following the manufacturer's instructions.

RIGHT
The Golden Poison Frog is native to Colombia and is one of the most poisonous animals in the world!

Cars of Cuba Collection

CUBA

CUBAN FLAG

Cuba is home to a collection of super-cool looking classic cars. These cars look really great in silhouette, too, so this project uses multicolored car silhouettes to make a stunning piece of art. You could experiment with different shapes like flowers, hearts, robots, or even a cityscape full of rainbow buildings.

YOU WILL NEED

Printouts or photocopies of classic cars

Pencil

Scissors

Paint sample cards (available in paint shops)

Mat board cut to the size of the frame

Picture frame

Glue stick

1. Use the templates on page 125 to create your own classic car templates. You could trace them or make photocopies that you can cut out.

2. Use your templates to draw around and then cut out a random selection of different colored cars from your paint cards.

3. The best way to design a layout is to try positioning the car cutouts before you glue them onto the board. Remember to check where your frame edge finishes so that your cars don't get cut off when you frame them. Here, the cars are glued into a design of three rough columns, but you might want to do a random arrangements or straight lines.

4. Use your glue stick to glue the cars into place in your chosen design and then frame your picture!

fun fact

In Cuba today, one in eight of all cars is a pre-1960s American brand—Ford, Chevrolet, Cadillac, Chrysler, Packard, and other classic models.

"Bang on Time" Tin Can Drum

This tin-can drum is decorated with the Jamaican flag, but you could use your team colors or even some favorite photos to decorate your own tin drum. When you've finished you can experiment with different "drum sticks." You could use chopsticks, knitting needles, or even pencils.

1. Carefully peel the paper label off the can, try to keep it in one piece because this is your template for the decoration. Wash and dry your tin.

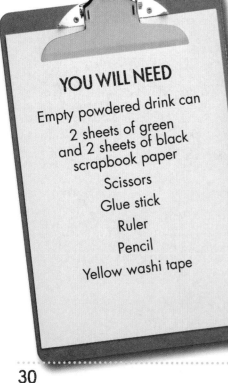

YOU WILL NEED

Empty powdered drink can

2 sheets of green and 2 sheets of black scrapbook paper

Scissors

Glue stick

Ruler

Pencil

Yellow washi tape

2. Use the template to cut out the green background color paper. You may need to stick two pieces together to get your paper long enough. Glue this onto the can.

3. Fold the paper template in half and cut. Fold one piece in half and then in half again. Turn the paper so that the center is top left (you can tell where the center is from the two folded sides joining in the corner). Using the ruler, draw a line from the bottom left to the top right corner. Cut along this line. This will give you a diamond-shaped template. Use the template to cut two diamonds out of the black scrapbook paper. Glue a diamond on each side of the tin. The top and bottom points will touch the tin edges and the side points will join up with each other.

JAMAICAN FLAG

4. Take a length of washi tape and position it so that it overlaps the green and the black papers. Use scissors to trim the tape at an angle to fit the tin.

fun fact

Traditionally, Jamaican steel drums were made from old oil barrels.

Un Gran Sombrero (A Great Hat) Paperweight

MEXICO

Clay is such a fun medium to use. Don't stop at making a sombrero paperweight for your desk. Why not try making a holder for your pencils or a coaster for your dad's coffee cup?

1. Roll a ball of clay (slightly larger than a golf ball) and place it on a cutting board. Flatten it with your palm and then, with a wet palm, flatten it further by pressing down and moving your palm in a circular motion. Continue until your clay is ⅛–⅜in (5–8mm) thick. Use the circular lid to imprint a circle in the clay and cut away any excess with a sharp knife, under adult supervision.

YOU WILL NEED

Air-drying clay
Cutting board
Large circular lid or cookie cutter
Bowl of water
Acrylic paints and paintbrush

2. Wet your fingertips and smooth the cut edges of the clay. Ensuring your fingers are wet, run them under the outside rim of the circle raising the outer edge to begin to form the hat brim.

3. While supporting the outer edge of the clay, run your wet fingers around the inside edge to complete molding the brim.

4. Take a large marble-sized piece of clay and roll it into a cylindrical shape with flat ends. While keeping one end flat, roll the other end gently between your fingers and the board to form a cone.

5. Using your fingers, dampen the flat end of your cylinder and press it down gently into the center of your clay circle.

6. Take another small ball of clay and roll it out between your fingers and the board to form a long "rope"-like piece that is thinner than a pencil. Don't worry if it breaks in parts as it can be joined to the clay by wetting the two ends and pressing them together. Rub wet fingers over the surface of your hat and, starting at the base of the cone, press the end of the rope against it and wind it up the cone, pressing it gently as you go until you reach the top.

MEXICAN FLAG

7. Break the end of the clay rope and press it neatly to join it to the main hat. Take another piece of rope and, this time, work your way from the base of the cone to the outer brim of the hat. When finished, press the rope down firmly with wet fingers to join and form a smooth, even surface— but take care not to erase all the lines of the rope joins. Allow your hat to dry completely.

8. Decide how you would like to decorate your sombrero (you may like to look at images in books or online for ideas), and then start painting!

fun fact

In Mexico, sombreros are made of different materials according to how wealthy the wearer is. Poor people's sombreros are usually made of straw. People who have more money wear sombreros made of felt.

"No Worries" Worry Dolls

PERU

These dolls are quick and easy to make. Acrylic paint is a lovely medium to work with, but small children might find it easier to use pens. You could make just one worry doll, but why not make a whole family of them with different faces and hairstyles?

YOU WILL NEED

Small paintbrush

Black, brown, red, and white acrylic paint

2 dolly clothespins

Toothpick

Scissors

Fabric scraps

Popsicle stick

White glue (PVA)

1. Paint round, white face shapes on your dolly clothespins. You may need two layers of paint. We've used paint for the hair here, but you could try gluing wool on top of the dolls instead. Use a toothpick dipped in acrylic to paint dainty details on the faces.

2. Cut out a piece of fabric 3 x 2½in (8 x 6cm). The size of the dolly pegs may vary, so line up the fabric with the pegs and check that it fits.

PERUVIAN FLAG

3. Use a popsicle stick to spread white glue onto the fabric. Fold over the bottom and top edges so that any fraying fabric is hidden and wrap the fabric tightly around your doll. Allow the glue to dry.

fun fact

In Peru, parents put worry dolls under their children's pillows if they are anxious about something. In the middle of the night, they remove the doll and the worry along with it!

"Stick with Me"
Magnet Pencil Tin

UNITED STATES OF AMERICA

Kids love to buy fridge magnets on their travels. There's one problem with this: kids don't have fridges! Make your own magnetic pencil can and you'll always have a home for your fridge magnets.

YOU WILL NEED

Clean, dry tin can

Black paint (you could use chalkboard paint)

Sponge paintbrush

Fridge magnets

1. Paint a clean, dry tin can and allow the paint to dry. If you're left with a sharp edge at the top, cover it with clear sticky tape.

fun fact

Times Square in New York City was renamed in April 1904 after the New York Times moved its headquarters to the newly erected Times Building — now called One Times Square.

2. Stick on your magnets and fill with pencils. You can change the magnets and move them around whenever you like.

USA FLAG

BELOW
The Statue of Liberty stands on Liberty Island in New York Harbor and was a gift from France to the United States.

Chapter 2
Europe

From the domes of St Basil's Cathedral in Moscow to the crisp lines of the Eiffel Tower in Paris, there is plenty of inspiration to be found in Europe. Make lovely, bright Dutch tulips (see page 64), or rock on with the Spanish castanets (see page 70)!

"Fa La La"
Paper Dolly Choir

Paper dollies are a timeless children's classic. Turn these dolls into a little choir with cool scrapbook paper clothes and sweet little faces.

AUSTRIA

ABOVE
Salzburg was one of the film locations for the 1965 musical The Sound of Music.

1. Take your tabloid size (A3) paper and cut it in half widthwise.

2. Take one of the halves of the paper and fold it into a concertina with four faces, each measuring 2in (5cm). This will make four dolls.

3. Flatten your concertina so that it is all folded together. Take the pencil and trace the "half dolly" shape on page 122 onto paper and then draw around it with the black pen on the flat end of your concertina. The center line of the doll should be on the fold, not the cut edge, the arm should be on the edge of the paper. Cut out the doll shape through all the layers of paper.

4. Repeat steps 2 and 3 with the second piece of paper. Now, glue your two dolly strips together by sticking them at the point of their unattached arms.

RIGHT
Many people go
skiing in the Alps
in Austria.

5. Draw simple
faces on your dolls.

6. Trace the dress and hairstyle
templates on page 122 onto paper
with the pencil. Use your paper
templates to cut out dresses and
hairstyles from colorful scrapbook
paper, then glue them onto the dolls.

Saving for a Snowy Day

FINLAND

We have used a curvy container to make this snowman but you could use any shape you have to design your own moneybox. A rectangle or a square would make a great robot. If you don't have a flap lid, a screw-top lid will work just as well. Make sure it has a large enough opening to get your money in and out.

1. Use the bread knife to cut approximately ⅛in (2mm) off the bottom of your Styrofoam ball to make a flat surface. Then cut an angled segment off the back to allow room for your flap to open. If you are using a screw-top lid, you do not need to cut off the second segment.

YOU WILL NEED

Bread knife

2½ (65mm) Styrofoam ball

Plastic container with a flip or screw-top lid

Black and white paint

Plastic lid (we used the lid from a cream container but a lid from a small jar would work)

Soft drink lid (black, if you have one)

Glue gun (craft glue can eat away the foam so use a glue gun or PVA)

6 small buttons

1 large or medium–sized button

Scissors

Brown and orange pipe cleaners

5 small brads (you can add more if you wish)

2 large brads

Your choice of fabric or ribbon

Pinking shears

2. Paint your Styrofoam ball and plastic container white and your lids black. The paint may not take properly on the first coat, so allow it to dry thoroughly and apply a second coat.

3. Place the lid back on your container and tighten it, locate the front, and glue your buttons down the center of your snowman's body.

4. Ask an adult to use the end of a pair of scissors to make a ⅛-in (2–3-mm) hole on your plastic container where you would like your snowman's arms to be. Cut two 3⅛-in (8-cm) pieces from your brown pipe cleaner and thread them into the holes. Secure with glue and bend as desired.

5. With the lid on the container, glue the foam ball onto the lid—make sure the flap can still open. Glue the two black lids together to form a top hat, and then glue it in place on the top of your foam ball. Insert your brads to form a mouth and eyes. Cut a 1½-in (4-cm) piece of orange pipe cleaner, fold it in half, and push the ends into your Styrofoam ball to make a nose.

FINNISH FLAG

6. Cut a 1½-in (4-cm) wide piece of fabric (you could use ribbon) with pinking shears and fold it in half. Secure it to the back of your lid and then wrap around the front. Fold one side as shown and then overlap the other and secure. You could also add a button for decoration. Now all you need to do is start saving!

"Ooh La La"
Pretty Parisian Embroidery

FRANCE

Embroidery can seem a bit daunting but all you really need to know are a few simple stitches and how to tie a good knot! Curve stitching is a wonderful way of creating curves with thread by using simple straight stitches. If you thread some pretty ribbon through the top of your embroidery hoop, your Eiffel Tower is framed and ready to hang on your wall! Some embroidery is very precise and requires exact stitches, but with this one you can have fun! Aside from the Eiffel Tower, you can play around with the birds, bushes, and trees until you like the way it looks.

YOU WILL NEED

Sharp pencil

8¼-in (21-cm) diameter side plate, or a plate about 2-in (5-cm) larger in diameter than the embroidery hoop

Fabric scrap—lightweight printed cotton is used here

Pinking shears or scissors

6¼-in (16-cm) diameter embroidery hoop, or choose a size you like

Paper

Ruler

Embroidery cotton in gray, black, green, and yellow/brown

Embroidery needle with a large eye

3ft (1m) of ribbon

SEWING THE EIFFEL TOWER:

REPUBLIQUE ·015· FRANCAISE

1. Take the pencil and draw around the plate onto the fabric. Cut out the circle with pinking shears or scissors.

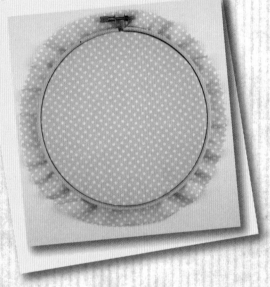

2. Take the embroidery hoop, slightly undo the screw on top, and separate the hoops. Place the fabric over the smaller hoop and trap it in place by putting the larger hoop on top. As you tighten the hoop, make sure the fabric is as taut and smooth as you can make it.

3. The Eiffel Tower is the only element that needs to be drawn before stitching. You can either trace the template on page 124 or draw it according to the following instructions: On a piece of paper draw a triangle 2 (bottom) x 2¾ x 2¾in (5 [bottom] x 7 x 7cm). Draw dots every ¼in (6mm) up the long sides of the triangle, and number your dots as shown. With this curved stitching you will leave out the top dot of the triangle. This means that two threads will form the top of the triangle. Draw a dot 1in (2.5cm) above these two points. Draw another dot ½in (1.5cm) above this one. Using a sharp pencil, punch out tiny holes where the dots are. This will be the stencil for the Eiffel Tower design.

Place the stencil over the fabric. The Eiffel Tower should be in the center, the top dot about ⅜in (1cm) from the top of the hoop. Use your pencil to lightly mark the dots onto the fabric. Make a knot in a piece of gray cotton and start at the top right hole number 1, threading up through the hole from the back. Thread into the left side number 1. From the back push your needle into the number 2 right-hand hole and then through and up to the left-side hole number 2. Continue this process—working from side to side—until you arrive back at the top left number 9. From here, thread up through the back of the number 1 right hole and thread into point A. Thread through the back of top number 9, thread into A, and then out through point B and then finally back again to A. Knot and trim excess cotton.

SEWING THE BIRDS:

6. The tiny black birds in flight are very simple to sew. Knot your black cotton and push the needle through where you want one of the birds. Make a ¼-in (5-mm) stitch from the top of the wing to the center of the bird. Push the needle through the fabric at the other wing tip and bring back into the center. You can either tie a knot in between birds or simply carry on to the next bird.

SEWING THE BUSHES:

7. The green bushes are sewn in running stitch. Knot your cotton, push it through the fabric, and make tiny stitches in wiggly lines. These stitches are about ⅛in (3mm) long. You could vary them or make them longer if you prefer. You can sketch your bushes lightly with pencil before sewing if you like.

SEWING THE PATH:

8. The pathway is sewn with long stitches that gradually get shorter as they go down. Knot your cotton and push the needle through the fabric just inside the foot of the Eiffel Tower. Use one long stitch to get to the other foot. Make a tiny stitch down and slightly in and stitch to the other side. Repeat until you are happy with your path.

9. Turn your hoop over and gently tuck the fabric edge into the frame—you may want to use a blunt knife to help you do this. Thread your ribbon through the top of the embroidery hoop and tie a knot. You could cut the ribbon short, tie it in a bow, or leave it long as a feature.

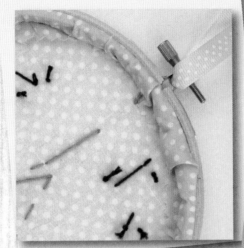

FRENCH FLAG

fun fact

Did you know that Gustav Eiffel designed not only the Eiffel Tower but also the Statue of Liberty in New York?

"Give Them a Hand" Paper Wreath Crown

GREECE

Wreath crowns are really quick and easy to make and great for dressing up. You could customize this idea and make a fairy crown in pink or silver and cover it with sequins and glitter. Or why not make a king's crown in gold card and add jewels to it?

GREEK FLAG

1. Draw around your hand onto the white paper and cut it out. This is your template.

YOU WILL NEED

Pencil or a pen

Piece of white paper

Green construction paper

Thin black card, letter (A4) size

Scissors

Glue stick

2. Draw around your template onto the green construction paper. Eleven hands are used to make the wreath shown here, but you could use more or fewer depending on your head size.

3. Take the black card and, using the scissors, cut out two strips 1½in (4cm) wide along the long side of the card. Glue them together with a 1-in (2-cm) overlap to make a long strip. Wrap the strip around your head and mark where the two ends overlap with a pencil. Allow for a 1-in (2-cm) overlap, trim one end, and then glue the strips together to form the crown shape.

4. Take one of your green paper hands and glue the palm of the hand onto the crown shape. Make sure you don't glue the fingers down. Glue the next hand so that the fingers overlap the back of the first glued hand. Repeat with the rest of your hands until you have gone all the way round your crown.

fun fact

Did you know that during the parade of nations at the opening ceremony of each Olympic Games, Greece always enters first? This is because Greece was the country where the Olympics were invented.

"Tip Top" Op Art Greeting Card

Op art is a style of art that often uses geometric shapes, like circles and squares, to produce different effects. For this project, you can layer your tissue paper to make different hues and varying tones. The hue is the color and the tone means how light or dark that color is.

HUNGARY

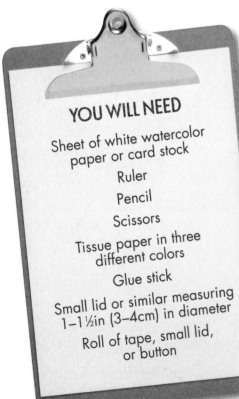

YOU WILL NEED

Sheet of white watercolor paper or card stock

Ruler

Pencil

Scissors

Tissue paper in three different colors

Glue stick

Small lid or similar measuring 1–1½in (3–4cm) in diameter

Roll of tape, small lid, or button

1. Measure your card stock with the ruler, mark it, and cut it so that it measures 9½ x 9½in (24 x 24cm). Then fold the card in half.

fun fact

Op art stands for optical art. It is a style of art that uses optical illusions. A Hungarian artist named Victor Vasarely was one of the first op artists.

2. Cut out a range of tissue paper squares measuring 1½ x 1½in (4 x 4cm). There will be a grid of nine squares in your card design, but because you will be layering the tissue paper you will need about 20 in total to produce a great effect.

HUNGARIAN FLAG

3. Now cut out a range of different colored tissue paper circles with a diameter of 1–1½in (3–4cm) to fit in the squares. See if you can find a roll of tape, a lid, or a button that fits to draw around to make it easier. Again, cut out about 20.

4. Tissue paper can be tricky to glue because it tears easily. Gently move the glue stick across your tissue paper shapes and stick them onto the card. Allow to dry.

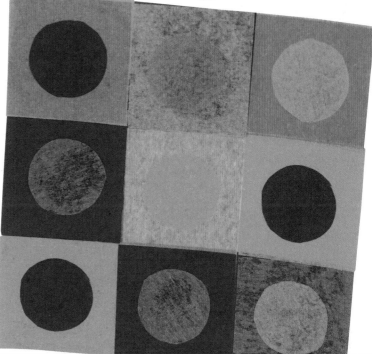

"Three (Salt Dough) Coins in the Fountain"

ITALY

YOU WILL NEED

FOR THE DOUGH:
1½ cups (7½oz/225g) of plain flour
½ cup (5oz/140g) of fine table salt
1 tablespoon of cooking oil
⅔ cup (5½fl oz/160ml) of water

Cup measure
Mixing bowl and spoon
Rolling pin
Parchment paper
Baking sheet
2 cookie cutters in different sizes
Paintbrush
Spatula
Cooling rack
Metallic acrylic paint in silver and gold

Salt dough is great. It's cheap and quick to make, and the best bit is that it uses ingredients most people keep in the pantry. You can use it to make these play coins, or why not make Christmas tree ornaments, too?

ABOVE
The Fontana de Trevi—the Trevi Fountain—is one of many magnificent landmarks in Rome in Italy.

1. Mix your salt dough ingredients together in a bowl and knead them until you have made a smooth dough. Set your oven to 248°F (120°C/Gas ½).

ITALIAN FLAG

fun fact

If you throw a coin into the Trevi Fountain in Rome, myth has it that one day you will return to Rome.

2. On a floured surface roll out your dough until it's about ¼in (7mm) thick. For a really smooth finish, roll out your dough between two pieces of parchment paper.

3. Line your baking sheet with parchment paper. Use your cookie cutters to cut rounds out of your dough in both sizes and then transfer them to your baking sheet.

4. Using the wrong end of the paintbrush to make indentations, mark a design on the coins. Here, holes were punched around the outside edge and the small coins have been marked with the number 5 and the large ones with a 10.

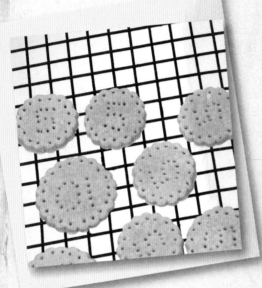

5. Bake the coins in the oven for two hours or until your coins are hard. Ask an adult to help you with the oven and the hot baking sheets. Transfer the coins to your cooling rack with the spatula and leave them to cool down.

6. Pick a different paint color for each denomination (number) coin. Paint them and allow the paint to dry.

NETHERLANDS

NETHERLANDS FLAG

Easy Peasy
Felt Tulips

We love the simplicity of these tulips but you could be more adventurous and make flowers like roses or daffodils. Try picking up leaves in the garden or the park and use them as templates for different leaf shapes.

1. Use the the leaf and tulip templates on page 124 to make your own leaf and flower templates from paper. You could trace or photocopy the templates.

YOU WILL NEED

(makes 4 flowers plus 4 leaves)

Paper and pen

1 piece red felt

1 piece pink felt

1 piece green felt

Scissors

8 green pipe cleaners

2. Draw around your templates on the pieces of felt until you have two red flowers, two pink flowers, and four green leaves. Cut them out.

3. Bend your flowers in half from side to side and make two tiny ⅛-in (5-mm) snips ¾in (2cm) from the top and bottom. Repeat this with the leaves.

4. Feed your pipe cleaners through the holes in the felt flowers and leaves to make the flower stems.

BELOW
Tulips are the unofficial national flower of the Netherlands.

"Let It Snow" St Basil's Snow Globe

There is something special about snow globes, which makes them hard to resist. Tipping them upside down creates a magical world as the glitter swirls around. These twisted polymer clay domes look so much like St Basil's Cathedral in Moscow that you could almost imagine you were there.

YOU WILL NEED

Polymer clay in red and blue

Small baby food jar with lid

Baking parchment on a baking tray

Boiled and cooled water

Iridescent glitter

Glycerine

Strong glue or a glue gun

RIGHT
Moscow's Red Square, the Kremlin (where the president of Russia lives), and St Basil's Cathedral.

1. Warm the red polymer clay by rolling it between your hands. Take a piece about the size of a marble and roll it into a ball. Take another piece of red clay, again about the size of a marble, but this time mold it into a mini pointed dome shape. Set them aside. Roll a length of red clay into a tube about 7 x ¼in (18 x 0.5cm) long, and then cut it into six equal-size pieces. Wash your hands, because the clay can stain them.

RUSSIAN FLAG

2. Now make another long tube with the blue clay—roll the clay in your hands to soften it up before using it. Cut it into six pieces. Finally, take a piece of blue clay the size of a large marble, roll it into a ball, and then flatten it gently to make a disk. Check that it fits into the lid of the jar, leaving a little space around the edge so that the jar can still be screwed on.

St Basil's Cathedral in Moscow, Russia's capital city.

3. Take the red ball of clay and press it lightly with your palm to create a flat base for the swirled dome. Take one of the lengths of red clay and press it onto the base. Do the same with a length of blue clay, and then continue around the base, adding lengths of clay in alternating colors until the base is covered. Gently twist the lengths of clay at the top to create the swirled effect. Keep twisting until the clay breaks and forms a point.

4. Place your swirled dome onto the disk of clay in the lid of the jar, and take the tiny red dome you made in step 1 and place it next to your two-color dome. Check that they will fit into your jar by placing the jar over them. Place your domes and disk on a piece of baking parchment on a baking sheet and bake them according to the manufacturer's instructions.

5. Clean and dry your jar. Almost fill the jar with water and add a teaspoon of glitter and a teaspoon of glycerine to the water. Remember, you need to leave enough room for your domes!

6. Glue the disk of polymer clay into the lid of your jar. Then glue your domes onto the disk and allow the glue to dry. Screw the lid on as tightly as you can and your snow globe is finished!

Click-clack Button
Castanets

Who doesn't love a noisy toy? These castanets make a lovely sound and fit neatly into your hand. You could customize them with your name, or a picture of a favorite sport team.

fun fact

Castanets got their name from the Spanish word for chestnut, which is "castaña." Traditionally, castanets were made from chestnut wood.

YOU WILL NEED

Mat board
Cutting knife, ruler, and cutting mat
Scissors for scoring
Scrapbook paper
Glue stick
4 buttons
Strong glue (UHU)

1. Measure the mat board with the ruler and cut a piece measuring 8 x 1½in (20 x 4cm) on the cutting mat. Ask an adult to use the cutting knife for you.

2. With the sharp edge of the scissors, score a line down the middle of the board at the 4in (10cm) mark. Gently fold the board in half at the score line. This will be the outside of the castanet.

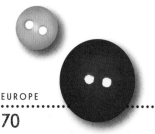

3. Cut out two pieces of 4 x 1½-in (10 x 4-cm) patterned or decorated paper, or you could paint or draw directly onto the board to decorate your castanet. Using the glue stick, glue your paper onto the same side of the mat board that you scored.

SPANISH FLAG

4. Turn the mat board over and, using the strong glue, stick a button on each end. Remember, they have to meet when the castanet is closed to make the click-clack sound!

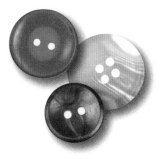

5. Now make another castanet so that you have a pair.

"Deck the Halls" Magazine Tree

SWEDEN

You really only need one thing to make this simple tree: a magazine! Each page is folded three times so you'll need a bit of patience, too. You could glue glitter to the page edges and turn your tree into a Christmas ornament, or spray it orange and red for a fall table arrangement.

YOU WILL NEED
A magazine with the cover removed
Paper clip

1. Take the first right-hand page of the magazine and fold the top corner down to form a triangle shape.

2. Take the triangle you have just folded and fold it over again so that the edge of the triangle lines up with the spine of the magazine.

SWEDISH FLAG

3. Turn the bottom edge of the triangle up so that it is level with the bottom of the page.

4. Repeat this until you have done it to every page in the magazine. Use your paper clip to join the front and back pages together.

RIGHT
Christmas in Stockholm, which is Sweden's capital city. This is Gamla Stan, the old town area of the city.

"Spin Me Round" Dancing Dervish

With some simple gluing and sewing you can be twirling your own dancing dervish. But don't stop there, use this simple design to create a ballerina or a caped super hero! You are limited only by your imagination.

TURKEY

ABOVE
The Blue Mosque in Istanbul, the largest city in Turkey. But Istanbul is not the capital—this honor goes to Ankara.

YOU WILL NEED

Ruler
Round balsa wood ½in (12.5mm) in diameter
Bread knife
Orange pipe cleaner
Toothpick or bamboo skewer
Scissors
White cotton fabric
Small piece of brown felt
Glue
¾in (20.5mm) Styrofoam ball
Black marker pen
Needle and thread
Black ribbon

1. Cut a 12-in (30-cm) piece of the balsa wood. This can be done easily with a bread knife—just ask an adult for help. Fold a pipe cleaner in half and place it approximately ⅜in (1cm) in from the end of your balsa rod. Wrap it around twice, and then twist to secure.

TURKISH FLAG

2. Break your toothpick in half (or cut approximately ¾in/2cm from the sharp end of a bamboo skewer) and insert it into the top of your balsa wood at the center point. Leave ⅜in (1cm) protruding.

3. Cut out two pieces of your white fabric. The first piece needs to be 7in (18cm) wide by 16¾–17¾in (40–45cm) in length, if you cut along the selvage of the fabric (the selvage is the natural edge of the fabric), this saves you from having to hem. The second piece should be 2⅜ x 5½in (6 x14cm). Take the second, smaller piece and fold and iron the edges running the length of the fabric. Then fold it in half lengthwise and then in half widthwise. Make an angled cut of ⅛in (2mm) at the corner fold of the fabric; this will leave a small hole in the center of the fabric piece when you open it out.

4. Cut a 3½ x 1½in (9 x 4cm) piece of brown felt. Glue along one long and one short side. Place your foam ball half on and half off the felt, roll it up toward the glued edge, and secure.

5. Place a small dab of glue around the toothpick inserted in the balsa wood. Drape the small piece of white fabric over the top of the wood, allowing the toothpick to go through the hole you cut previously. Press the foam ball onto the toothpick and let the glue dry. With a black marker, draw two curves on the foam ball to represent the dancer's closed eyes.

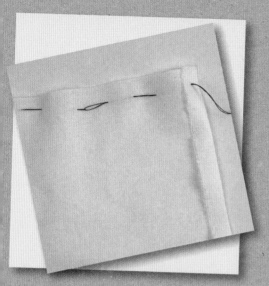

6. Taking your large fabric piece, fold and iron the short ends over to form a hem. Thread a needle with around 8in (20cm) of cotton. Sew long loose stitches along the non-selvage length. Gather the fabric together to form your skirt.

7. Tie your gathered skirt around the balsa wood and the edge of the other fabric, making sure it is gathered evenly and secured tightly. Wrap a piece of black ribbon around the gather to form a belt and either glue or tie it off. With the black marker, draw the tips of shoes onto the balsa wood at the same length the skirt hem falls. You can now start twirling!

BELOW
The Whirling Dervishes

fun fact

The Whirling Dervishes are a popular tourist attraction in Turkey. Did you know that they perform an Islamic holy dance? As they spin, they represent the Earth revolving on its axis while orbiting the sun.

"One is Amused"
Royal Family Wooden Spoon Puppets

Wooden spoon puppets can be as basic or as elaborate as you like. You could add clothes or wool hair, but the real fun starts when you add the voices!

YOU WILL NEED
Acrylic paint
Wooden spoons
Fine paintbrushes
Black fine-tip pen

UNITED KINGDOM

ABOVE
Buckingham Palace in London, the capital city of the United Kingdom.

1. Paint an oval face shape on the spoon. If you want to use a skin color, experiment by mixing small amounts of yellow, red, and brown into the white paint.

2. When the paint is dry, add the features of the face with a black pen.

BRITISH FLAG

3. Paint on the details of your puppet's character. You could paint on hair, hats, crowns, ears—any features you like to make your character come alive. Here, there is a queen, a corgi, and a guard to give you some ideas. Maybe you can think of some other London faces? How about a police officer, a princess, or a Beefeater?

fun fact

Do you know how to tell if the Queen is at Buckingham Palace? If she is in residence, the Royal Standard flies above the palace. When she is not there, the famous red, white, and blue Union Jack flag flies instead.

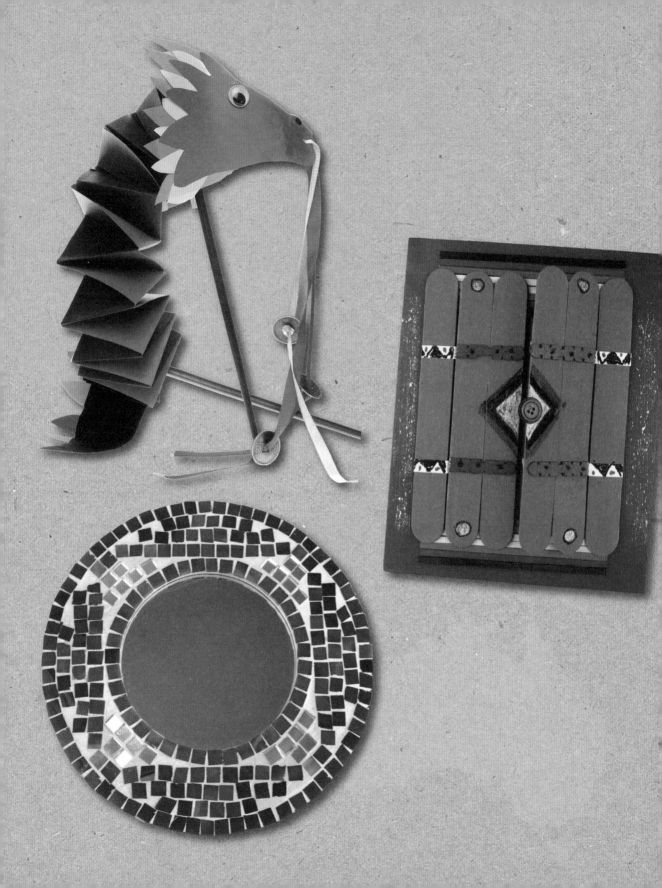

Chapter 3
Asia and Oceania

This part of the world has clear sunshine and big blue skies. In fact, Japan is often referred to as the "land of the rising sun"! Chase away the gray skies with our dragon puppet (see page 86), or add a touch of color to clothes or a bag with quirky sushi brooches (see page 94).

Forever Sydney
Memory Jar

AUSTRALIA

Keeping tickets and tiny treasures is a wonderful way to keep your travels alive. It doesn't take long to turn a glass jar into a memory capsule to keep for ever. You could also make these to celebrate birthdays or school years.

YOU WILL NEED

Map
Clean glass jar with lid
Pencil
Scissors
Glue brush
White glue (PVA or `Mod Podge)
Small souvenirs

1. Take your map of Sydney and your jar lid and, with the pencils, trace around the lid on the piece of map. Cut out the disk of map. Using the brush, glue the piece of the map onto the lid and leave to dry.

fun fact

The Sydney Opera House is covered in more than one million white and cream tiles.

2. Paint a layer of glue on top of the map to protect it and add gloss. When the glue dries it will be clear.

3. Fill your jar with treasures and souvenirs from your travels.

BELOW LEFT
The Sydney Opera House is one of the busiest performing arts centers in the world.

AUSTRALIAN FLAG

Tame Your Dragon

CHINA

Chopsticks can be tricky to use sometimes, but not with this craft! Have fun decorating your own dragon puppet and use the chopsticks to teach him to perform a Chinese Dragon Dance, or take him with you on some magical adventures.

ABOVE
At Chinese New Year and other special occasions, the celebrations often include dancing with life-size dragon puppets.

YOU WILL NEED

Glue

Red, black, yellow, and orange origami paper

Scissors

Ruler

Chopsticks

Cardboard

Red, yellow, and orange ribbon

Chinese lucky coins (available to buy in party supplies stores)

Pair of craft eyes

1. Glue a sheet of red origami paper to the back of a yellow sheet to create one double-sided piece of paper. Cut the double-sided sheet and your black sheet of paper into 2-in (5-cm) strips. You should end up with five strips of each.

2. Take one black paper strip and glue the end of it to the end of a colored strip at a right angle. Begin folding the strips on top of one another—continue to do this, gluing more strips onto the ends of each piece as they come to an end. Continue until you have a nice length of "chain" for your dragon's body. Glue the end pieces down.

3. Cut four 2-in (5-cm) wide lengths of black paper. Fold the end of each piece down by 1¼in (3cm). Set aside two pieces to make your dragon's head. Cut out the shape of your dragon's tail (see the template on page 126) on both pieces of black paper. Now cut out some spike shapes from the colored paper and glue them down on one side of the tail shape, following the shape of the dragon's tail. Glue the other black tail piece to the same side as the spikes. Be sure to leave the folded ends of your paper unglued because they will be used to attach the tail to your dragon's body.

4. Glue a chopstick to the center of one end of the dragon's body. Then glue the two black flaps of your dragon's tail on either side of the chopstick, attaching them to the body.

CHINESE FLAG

5. Using the template of the dragon's head (see page 126), cut the shape out in cardboard. Use the cardboard shape to cut out six head-shaped pieces in orange, red, and yellow—alter the position of the spikes of the dragon's head slightly for each color, so that they will all be visible when they are glued together. You will need a layer of three colors for each side of the dragon's head. Add eyes and a nose to each side of the top red template.

6. Using the two spare black strips of paper you cut out earlier, glue three pieces of ribbon to the center of the non-folded end. Then glue the layers of the dragon's face on each side. Attach a chopstick and attach the dragon's head to the body just as you did for the tail. Knot some Chinese good luck coins onto the ribbon and you are ready to start taming him!

"Tile the Taj" Mosaic Mirror

INDIA

The Taj Mahal features some amazing examples of mosaic tiling. We have chosen a simple design inspired by the Taj Mahal, and the mirror represents the reflection pool at the front of this iconic building.

YOU WILL NEED

Wooden mirror from craft/hardware store

Acrylic paint and paintbrush

Mosaic glue paste

Mini pre-cut mosaic tiles in assorted colors

White super-fine grout

Water

Squeegee

Soft cloth

Clear sealer

1. Remove the mirror and backing from the frame. Paint the outer and inner rims of your wood frame in acrylic paint, as these surfaces will still be visible after you have tiled.

2. Using some inspiration from books and photographs of the Taj Mahal plan out your design on the frame. To make things easier you could divide your design into quarters and mark out the different parts of the design with a pencil. Don't forget to check where your hanging hook is placed on the back of your frame so that the design will hang correctly.

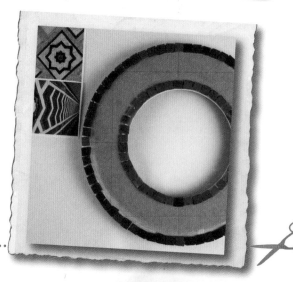

INDIAN FLAG

3. Glue each tile in place and allow to dry for 24 hours.

4. Mix your grout with water according to the manufacturer's instructions and use your squeegee to spread the grout over the mosaic and fill in the spaces between the tiles until they're even and smooth. Allow the grout to dry slightly, and then wipe off the excess with a soft, damp cloth. Allow the grout to completely dry, and then seal the mosaic with clear sealer to protect it. Now it is time to replace the mirror and backing and hang your work in pride of place!

fun fact

The Taj Mahal has a reflecting pool, which offers visitors a perfect reflection of the symmetrical building.

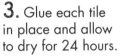

Personalized Shadow Puppet Theater

YOU WILL NEED

FOR THE PUPPET:

Scissors

Letter-size (A4), full-length printed photo of yourself

Black card or paper

Strong glue or tape

Wooden spoon

Pencil

FOR THE THEATER:

Cheap picture frame, tabloid size (A3) or larger

Parchment paper

Glue stick

Strong glue

2 building blocks

Flashlight

INDONESIA

Shadow puppetry is an ancient form of storytelling used in many different countries, including Indonesia. Tell your own story by making a puppet of yourself to use in your own shadow puppet theater.

1. Cut yourself out of the photograph and, using this as a template, cut another you out of black card or paper. Alternatively, use the templates on page 123.

2. Tape or glue your wooden spoon on to the back of the black cut-out.

3. Use the frame's backing board as a template to cut a piece of parchment paper to fit behind the frame. You could glue two pieces together to make a larger size if needed. Glue around the edges of the inside of the frame, using strong glue, and press the paper onto it.

INDONESIAN FLAG

4. Paint your building blocks to match the frame, and then glue them onto the back of the frame in the bottom corners at right angles. This will form the stand. To use your shadow puppet theater, shine a flashlight behind your frame and work your puppets in front of the light so that their shadows fall on the screen. Now you can create your own stories!

"Fishing for Compliments" Sushi Brooches

These felt brooches come together really quickly and all you need to do is cut, roll, and stick! Funk up an outfit or pin them onto a bag.

YOU WILL NEED

Scissors
Felt in pink, white, black, pale green, and orange
Strong glue (UHU)
2 brooch backs

fun fact

Did you know that, traditionally, the rice used in sushi was only there to help ferment the raw fish and was thrown away before the fish was eaten?

FOR THE SUSHI ROLL BROOCH:

1. Cut the felt into the following lengths:
Pink and white: ⅝ x 10¾in (1.5 x 27cm)
Black: ⅝ x 5¼in (1.5 x 13cm)
Pale green: ⅝ x 1in (1.5 x 2.5cm)

2. Start by rolling the pink felt into a tight coil. Dab a small amount of glue on to the end of the strip to stick it down. Fold the green strip in half and stick it at the end of the pink coil. Now stick on the white strip and roll it around the whole thing. Glue the end of the white felt down, and then add the black felt, wrapping it all around and sticking it in place.

3. Glue on the brooch back and allow the glue to dry.

LEFT
Sushi is a Japanese food made of rice and other ingredients—usually raw fish or other seafood.

ABOVE
Mount Fuji is on Honshu Island and
is the highest mountain in Japan.

FOR THE SHRIMP SUSHI BROOCH:

1. Cut out a piece of 9½ x 2in (24 x 5cm) white felt and an orange shrimp shape, about 2 in (5cm) long.

JAPANESE FLAG

2. Start by rolling the white felt into a tight coil along the shorter edge. Use a dab a of glue to stick the white felt coil down, and then glue the shrimp shape onto the finished roll.

3. Glue on the brooch back and allow the glue to dry.

Yarn Bombed "Baaaaaaa" Stool

Yarn bombing is a type of street art or graffiti, which uses yarn rather than paint. This project uses rainbow yarn, which gives a fabulous multicolored effect. You don't use glue in this project, so like yarn bombing, nothing is permanent! You can wrap yarn around anything. Try your pencil pot for a smaller project, or the cover of a notebook.

NEW ZEALAND

YOU WILL NEED

Ball of rainbow yarn, wool or acrylic

Stool

Scissors

Blunt knife

1. Start wrapping the yarn about 2in (5cm) from the bottom of the leg. Hold a piece of yarn about 2in (5cm) long down the length of the stool leg, and then wrap the yarn tightly around the leg, trapping the end of the yarn.

fun fact

Did you know that New Zealand is one of the world's largest producers of wool?

2. Continue to wrap tightly until you reach about 1⅛in (3cm) from the top.

3. Tie a knot in the yarn and cut the yarn about 2in (5cm) from the knot. With a flat-bladed, blunt knife, push the end of the yarn under the wrapped yarn.

4. Repeat with the other three chair legs.

NEW ZEALAND
FLAG

"Frame Your Own Tribe" Door Photo Frame

SAUDI ARABIA

It is always fun to personalize things and the bright colors and geometric shapes used by Bedouin tribes that we're using here make this a fun and easy project.

ABOVE
Bedouins often travel with camels through the desert, as camels can go without water for long periods of time.

YOU WILL NEED

5 x 7in (12.5 x 18cm) wooden photo frame with a wide border (this one is 2⅛in/5.5cm wide)

Acrylic paints of your color choice

Paintbrush

Large craft sticks

Assorted small craft sticks

Quilling paper (or ribbon)

Ruler

Glue

Soft pastels

Spray varnish

1. Search books or the Internet for some inspiration on Bedouin art or tribal doors of the Middle East. Think about the colors and your design. Remove the backing and glass from your frame and paint it in your chosen base color.

2. You will need three large craft sticks for each door panel. The outer one on each side will remain fixed while the inner two will open to show your photograph. Paint all of the craft sticks according to your planned design—remember to paint both sides of your door panels.

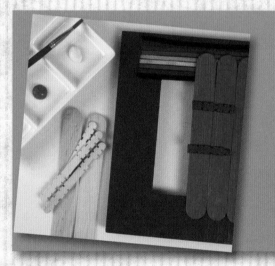

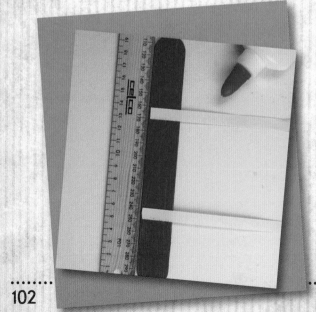

3. To assemble your door, take two pieces of quilling paper and, after measuring carefully, glue one one-third of the way down from the top and another one one-third from the bottom to the outer craft stick on your door.

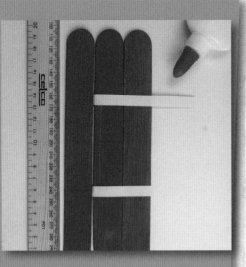

4. Flip that craft stick over, place the two remaining craft sticks under the quilling paper, and glue. Allow to dry.

SAUDI ARABIAN FLAG

fun fact
The word "Bedouin" comes from the Arab word "Bedou," which means "desert dweller." Bedouins traditionally live a nomadic lifestyle, herding sheep, goats, and camels.

5. Glue the door pieces onto your frame starting with the bottom pieces first.

6. Use your pastel crayons to decorate the door in some tribal designs. Spray with varnish to protect the design. Place your photo in the frame and display it proudly.

Simple Scissor Scarf

Learning how to make clothes for yourself opens up a whole new world of possibilities. You don't need to scour the shops for a special piece when you can make it at home! Turning something old like a t-shirt into a funky new scarf is so satisfying, and this one can be made in no time.

ABOVE
Dubai, the capital city of the United Arab Emirates.

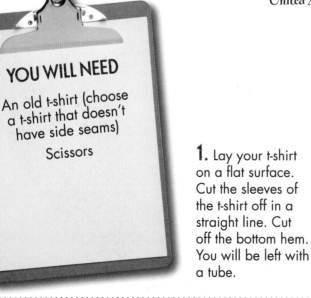

YOU WILL NEED

An old t-shirt (choose a t-shirt that doesn't have side seams)

Scissors

1. Lay your t-shirt on a flat surface. Cut the sleeves of the t-shirt off in a straight line. Cut off the bottom hem. You will be left with a tube.

2. Cut strips ¾in (2cm) apart across your tube of t-shirt fabric, from one side to the other. Stop cutting about 1½in (4cm) from one side edge.

fun fact

Many women in the United Arab Emirates wear a headscarf along with a niqab or another simple veil to cover all or most of their face when in public.

3. Open up your tube and grasp the side that you left uncut. Stretch your t-shirt between your hands so that the strips curl inward slightly.

Ha Long Bay
Juice Box Boats

VIETNAM

These sweet little boats are not just for show — they will float! You could make these for a play date and race them across a paddling pool or pond.

1. Drink the juice! Then remove the straw from your juice box and use the sticky tape to tape the hole shut securely.

YOU WILL NEED

Juice box
Sticky tape
2 bamboo skewers
Patterned scrapbook paper
Pencil
Ruler
Glass
Scissors
Glue stick
Small ball of adhesive putty or plasticine

2. Ask an adult to help you push the pointed end of a bamboo skewer through the juice box about 1 ¼ in (3cm) from the top and another one, 1 ¼ in (3cm) from the bottom. They should stick through the bottom of the box by about ¾ – 1 ¼ in (2–3cm).

fun fact

Ha Long Bay is a beautiful bay in Vietnam. Its name literally means "descending dragon bay." In Vietnamese culture, the dragon represents the universe, life, existence, and growth.

VIETNAMESE FLAG

3. On patterned scrapbook paper, draw two rectangles measuring 3 x 6in (8 x 15cm). Place the glass on the right-hand corner of one of the rectangles and draw a curved corner—do this to the other rectangle, too. Cut both rectangles out with one curved corner.

4. Measure in by ⅜in (1cm) along the long edge of one of the rectangles and fold along the line. Glue along the fold and press one of your bamboo skewers into the crease. Make sure the paper is positioned right at the top of your skewer. Do the same with the other rectangle and the other skewer.

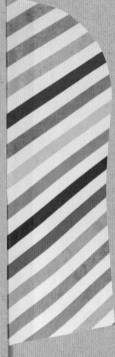

HANDY TIP

If your boat blows over, try sticking a small ball of adhesive putty or plasticine onto the bottom of the skewer to weigh it down.

Chapter 4
Africa

Africa is known around the world for its vibrant colors and bold designs. Why don't you try making your mark with a clay-bead necklet (see page 112), or wow your friends with the treasure hunt bottle (see page 110), inspired by the archeologist who discovered the tomb of a Pharoah in Egypt?

Howard's Treasure Hunt Bottle

Trinkets bought or found during our travels are a wonderful keepsake of experiences and places. Why not use them to make a discovery jar and have fun recalling all your travel tales?

EGYPT

ABOVE
The Pyramids in Egypt.

YOU WILL NEED

Clean cylindrical glass jar with lid

Collection of travel trinkets

Clean dry sand

fun fact

Howard Carter (9 May 1874 to 2 March 1939) was an English archeologist and Egyptologist who is known for discovering the tomb of the fourteenth-century BCE pharaoh, Tutankhamun.

1. Decide what you would like to put in your jar. You could use coins, a pebble, or a shell found on a walk, a souvenir key chain, ticket stubs, a passport photo—anything that holds memories of your trip.

EGYPTIAN FLAG

2. Place your trinkets in the bottom of the jar and then fill the jar with sand until it is three-quarters full.

3. Now have fun turning your jar and rediscovering your trinkets. Give your friends a try and see if they can find all your hidden treasures!

Worldly Wisdom Clay Bead Necklet

Clay beads have been made in Africa for thousands of years. Air-drying clay is quick and easy to use, and the great thing is, you don't need any special equipment. We've used the Adinkra symbol for wisdom here, but you could stamp your name or initials on the necklet instead, or create your own symbol.

GHANA

YOU WILL NEED

Air-drying clay
Rolling pin (optional)
Blunt knife
Leather lace
Biro pen
Paintbrush

1. Break off a piece of clay about the size of a walnut and use your hand to flatten the clay until it is about ¼in (5mm) thick. You can use a rolling pin to do this.

fun fact

Adinkra are visual symbols originally created by the Akan people of Ghana. They are used in art and architecture, pottery, and advertising.

2. Trim the edges off your clay with the blunt knife so that you are left with a neat rectangle. This one measures 2 x 1in (5 x 2.5cm). You also need to allow room for a hole at one end of the rectangle to thread your leather lace through.

GHANAIAN FLAG

3. Stamp your design on the rectangle. The end of a biro pen makes the large circles, and the end of the paintbrush makes the smaller ones. Use the paintbrush end to make a hole at one end large enough for the leather lace. Allow the clay to dry.

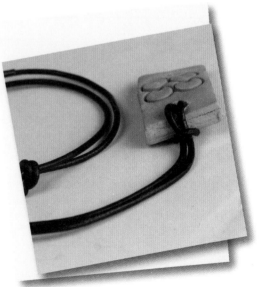

4. Thread both ends of the leather lace through the hole in the bead, then feed the ends back through the loop. Pull tight and your leather lace should be attached to the bead. Tie a knot at the end.

"Have a Drink on Me" Flag Coasters

These flag coasters are not only satisfying to make, they're also washable and waterproof, which makes them brilliant for drinks!

AFRICA

YOU WILL NEED

Square fusible bead tray

Fusible beads

Fusible bead ironing paper or parchment paper

Iron

1. First, look at lots of African flags and choose the flags that you want to use. Remember that flags are rectangular and your coasters are square. Flags with stripes work well because the design still looks good in a square shape.

2. Take the fusible bead tray and arrange the fusible beads on it in the design you have chosen. Cover the beads with a sheet of parchment paper and then ask an adult to fuse the beads together by ironing them. They should follow the manufacturer's instructions carefully.

RIGHT
Mount Kilimanjaro in Tanzania.

BELOW
Cape Town in South Africa.

From top to bottom, these coasters are made from the flags of Guinea, Tanzania, South Africa, and Nigeria.

Glossary

A3 PAPER
In many parts of the world, paper sizes are known by a letter and a number. Regular computer printer paper is called A4. Half this size is called A5, while double is called A3. In North America, the equivalent of A4 paper is letter size and the equivalent of A3 is tabloid size.

ACRYLIC PAINT
This is a water-soluble paint that you can use on lots of different surfaces, such as paper, canvas, and wood. It can be difficult to get out of clothing when it dries.

AIR-DRYING CLAY
Clay that dries without the need for a kiln or oven; it dries hard in the air.

BALSA WOOD
A lightweight wood that floats and is easy to cut. Balsa wood comes in sheets, dowels, and blocks and is available from craft, hobby, and hardware stores.

BAMBOO SKEWERS
Thin bamboo sticks used in cooking. Available in supermarkets.

BRAD
Decorative split pins. Available from stores where you can buy scrapbooking supplies.

BROOCH BACK
Pin backs that have a flat surface to fix decoration onto them.

ACRYLIC PAINT

BRADS

COFFEE FILTER PAPER

CRAFT EYES

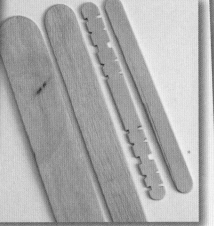

CRAFT STICKS

DOLLY CLOTHESPINS

CARD STOCK
Thicker than paper but thinner than mat board.

COFFEE FILTER PAPER
Made from crêpe paper and available in the coffee aisle at the supermarket.

CONSTRUCTION PAPER
Also known as sugar paper. It is a tough, rough-textured paper.

CRAFT EYES
Small plastic eyes that you can either sew or glue on to craft projects.

CRAFT STICK
A flat wooden stick that looks like a popsicle or lolly stick.

DIFFUSING PAPER
Diffusing paper has a fabric-like texture. Diluted paints spread through the paper, creating a beautiful effect.

DOLLY CLOTHESPINS
Old-fashioned wooden clothes pegs, now more commonly used for craft projects than for hanging out laundry.

EMBROIDERY COTTON
Embroidery cotton or embroidery floss is thicker than machine thread but thinner than yarn. It is used for hand embroidery.

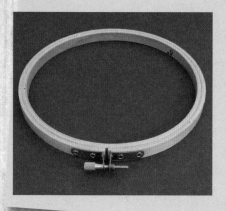

EMBROIDERY HOOP

FLORISTS' WIRE

EMBROIDERY COTTON & NEEDLE

EMBROIDERY NEEDLE
Embroidery needles come in a variety of sizes. Look for one with an eye that will fit your embroidery cotton or floss.

EMBROIDERY HOOP
Two hoops of bamboo or plastic that fit together, trapping a piece of fabric. They are used to keep fabric tight and flat when you are working on embroidery.

FELT
Non-woven cloth made by matting fibers together. Traditionally made of wool, craft felt is now more often made from synthetic fibers.

FLORISTS' WIRE
Comes in a variety of colors and sizes. Used for flower arranging and other art and craft projects.

FOOD DYE
Liquid or powder dye used in food.

FUSIBLE BEADS
These beads are made of plastic. You arrange a design on a special pegboard, and then iron the design to permanently fuse the beads together.

GLUE GUN
Electric tool that melts hot glue sticks to provide a glue with a strong bond.

GLUE STICK
Solid glue in a twist-up tube suitable for paper and card crafts.

GLYCERINE
A thick, colorless, odorless liquid.

PARCHMENT PAPER
Paper resistant to grease or oil. Used in cooking, it is available in supermarkets. It is also known as greaseproof or baking paper.

IRIDESCENT GLITTER
Iridescent glitter appears to change color as you look at it. Gemstones are naturally iridescent.

LEATHER LACE
A shoelace made of leather, used to make necklaces and bracelets.

MAT BOARD
A type of cardboard, usually with a color on one side and white on the other, used for mounting artwork in a frame.

MOD PODGE
Water-soluble craft glue. It comes in a variety of finishes from glossy to matt.

MOSAIC GLUE
A strong glue used to bond tiles to almost any surface.

MUSLIN BAG
Muslin is an unbleached, woven fabric. Craft stores sell items made from muslin to decorate. It is also known as calico.

ORIGAMI PAPER
There are various types of origami paper available for the art of origami. They must all be able to hold a crease.

PAINT SAMPLE CARDS
Small pieces of card with paint colors on them. These are free at hardware stores.

PASTELS
Crayons made from pure powdered pigment combined with a binder.

PINKING SHEARS
Scissors with zigzag blades; they are used to stop fabric raveling, or to add a decorative edge.

PIPE CLEANER
Also known as chenille stems. They are colored polyester fibers on a wire stem.

POLYMER CLAY
Synthetic clay that comes pre-colored. It is hardened in the oven.

PVA
White glue that can be cleaned up or diluted with water. It can also be painted onto craft items to give a glossy finish.

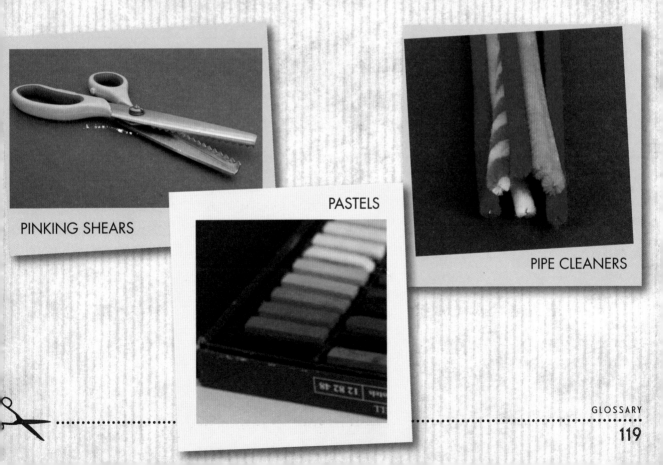

PINKING SHEARS

PASTELS

PIPE CLEANERS

STYROFOAM BALLS

SQUEEGEE

WASHI TAPE

QUILLING PAPER
Strips of paper that are rolled, shaped, and glued together to create decorative designs.

SCRAPBOOK PAPER
Printed paper available in beautiful designs. You can buy it in single sheets, or in books at craft stores.

SELVAGE
The self-finished edge of a piece of fabric.

SPONGE PAINTBRUSH
A sponge paintbrush has a piece of sponge in the place of bristles. You can use them for glue, varnish, or paint.

SPRAY VARNISH
Easy-to-use varnish that comes in an aerosol can. When you are using it, make sure you ventilate the area well to avoid the fumes.

SQUEEGEE
A tool with a smooth, flat, rubber blade. Used to apply grout to mosaic tiles.

STRONG GLUE
Solvent-based glue, stronger than PVA or white glue—for example, UHU.

STYROFOAM BALL
Lightweight craft material available in various shapes and sizes.

TILING GROUT
Used to fill the spaces between tiles or mosaics.

TISSUE PAPER
Lightweight paper available in a huge variety of colors.

WASHI TAPE
Decorative paper masking tape that originated in Japan. Available in craft stores.

WATER-BASED MARKERS
Washable pens used in art and craft.

YARN
Yarn can be made from natural or synthetic fibers. It can be used for various crafts, including knitting and crochet.

Templates

All the templates are provided at full size, so you just need to trace them off the page.

ANTARCTICA
page 16
full size

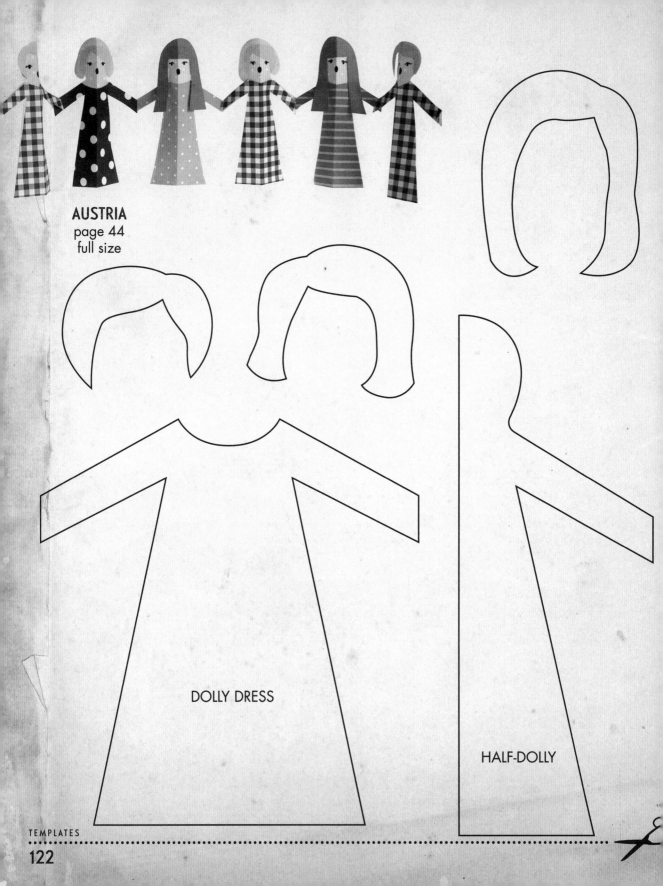

AUSTRIA
page 44
full size

DOLLY DRESS

HALF-DOLLY

INDONESIA
page 92
full size

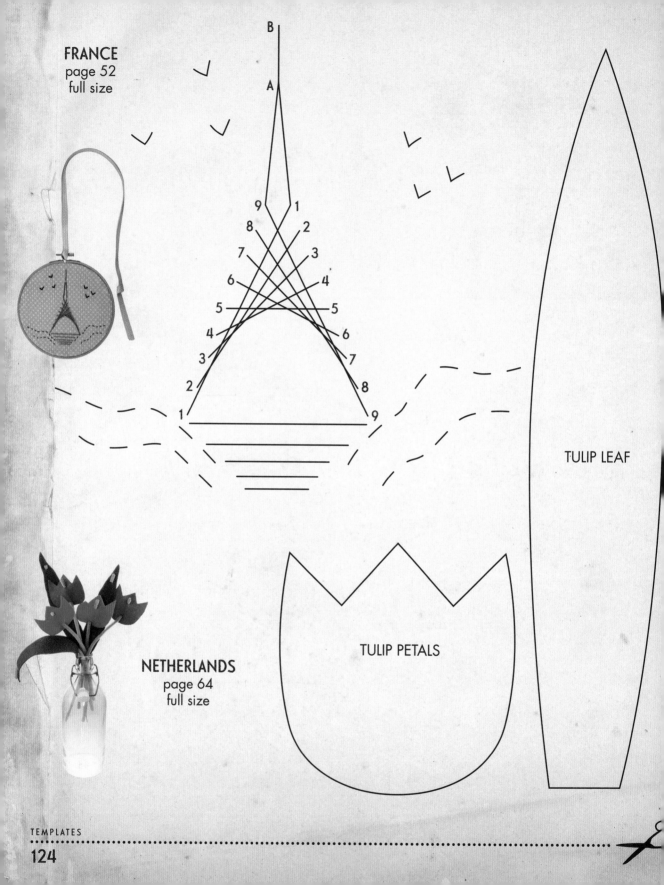

FRANCE
page 52
full size

B

A

9   1
8   2
7   3
6   4
5   5
4   6
3   7
2   8
1   9

TULIP LEAF

NETHERLANDS
page 64
full size

TULIP PETALS

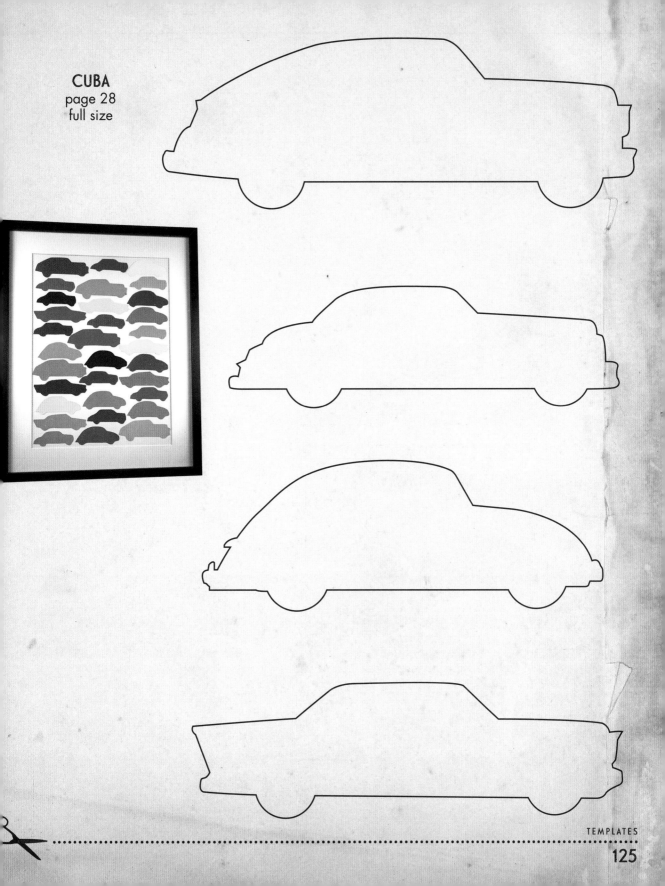

CUBA
page 28
full size

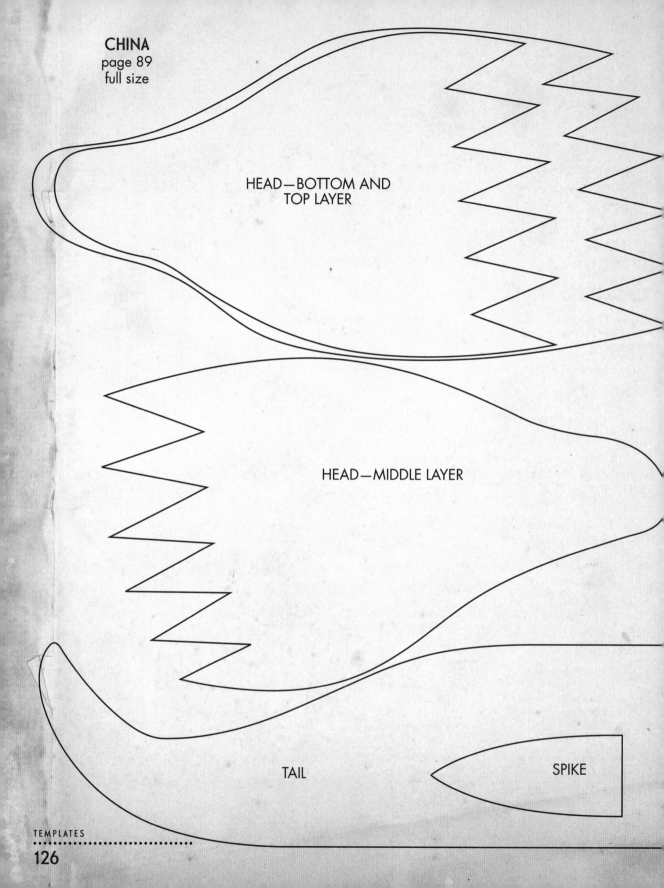

CHINA
page 89
full size

HEAD—BOTTOM AND
TOP LAYER

HEAD—MIDDLE LAYER

TAIL

SPIKE

Suppliers

AUSTRALIA

Bunnings Warehouse
www.bunnings.com.au

Cleverpatch
www.cleverpatch.com.au

Eckersley's Arts and Crafts
www.eckersleys.com.au

Lincraft
www.lincraft.com.au

Riot
www.riotstores.com.au

Spotlight
www.spotlight.com.au

Typo
shop.cottonon.com/shop/typo

US

A C Moore
www.acmoore.com

Create for Less
www.createforless.com

Darice
www.darice.com

Hobby Lobby
www.hobbylobby.com

Jo-Ann Fabric and Craft Stores
www.joann.com

Michaels
www.michaels.com

UK

Baker Ross
www.bakerross.co.uk

Homecrafts Direct
www.homecrafts.co.uk

Hobbycraft
www.hobbycraft.co.uk

John Lewis
www.johnlewis.co.uk

M is for make
www.misformake.co.uk

Yellow Moon
www.yellowmoon.org.uk

Index

Acknowledgments

Thanks to Cindy Richards for giving us the first interview, to Carmel Edmonds for helping us to navigate the world of publishing, to Phil Abadee for his unlimited generosity with freight, and to Kay Abadee for her advice. Thanks and love go to our parents, Ross and Sandra and Pat and Jon, our siblings, Amanda, Ben, Jane, and Susan, and our families and friends.

Picture credits
Illustrations, frames, and location photos listed below © iStockphoto.com and the following:

4X-image; albertc111; Aleksandar Kolundzija/vanillastring; Alex Keating; Andrea Romagnolo; Andrey_Kuzmin; Andrey Levitskiy/BARRI12; Andrjuss Soldatovs; asimetric; AVTG; bamlou; cofkocof; Damir Cudic; Dave White; desuza.communications/Colonel; dirk ercken; Dmitry Naumov/naumoid; DNY59; Edward Grajeda/grajte; emwar; Flavio Vallenari/argalis; FotografiaBasica; fototrav; Giorgio Fochesato/gioadventures; grahambedingfield; Halima Ahkdar; iconeer; ivanastar; Jamie Farrant; Joachim Angeltun/jangeltun; Joe Biafore; Joe Potato Photo; Kalin Eftimov/kaleff; Kalin Radoynov /koruin; Karim Hesham; kertlis; Kokkai Ng;

Linda Steward; Liz Leyden/SoopySue; Mark Stay/mstay; Markus Thomas Lienbacher/ dusteh; Mordolff; miniature; Mlenny Photography; Natasa Tatarin/nale; Nic Taylor; Oktay Ortakcioglu/craftvision; razberry; SantosJPN; SeanPavonePhoto; sndr; stock_art; studiocasper; Tahsin Aydogmus; uros ravbar; Valerie Loiseleux/Graffizone; wayra; WEKWEK; ZambeziShark

Ghana and Vietnam maps on pages 106/112 © Shutterstock/skvoor
Russia map on page 86 © Shutterstock/kaarsten